BECOMING A PUBLISHED AUTHOR

COURSE

EVERYTHING YOU WILL NEED TO PUBLISH YOUR BOOK

We've Done All The Hard Work...
You Just Have to Take This Content and Run with It

FILLED WITH TIPS, TEMPLATES AND FREEBIES

Copyright©2019 DYNASTY'S VISIONARY PUBLICATIONS. All Rights Reserved.

Have a great story but don't know how to get it out?

Learn How to Become a Published Author

From Research to Publishing, This Course will Guide You Through All the Steps!

Here's what you'll learn from this course:

- How to identify your genre and what sub-genres are in demand
- How to outline your content
- Where to look for inspiration
- Methods for getting your draft written quickly
- Which tools you can use to help with editing
- Where to find beta readers
- The exact steps you need to take to publish your new book

If you are ready to tell those stories you've always wanted to write, then order your course right now.

The information presented in this Product is intended to be for your educational and entertainment purposes only. We are not presenting you with a business opportunity or distribution. We are not making any claims as to the amount of income you may earn or a get rich scheme. Please use caution before signing to a publisher and seek the advice your own personal professional advisors, attorney and accountant.
Where figures are mentioned (if any), those income figures are anecdotal only.

Please do not construe any statement in this course and product as a claim or representation of guaranteed earnings. Testimonials and statements are not to be construed as claims. Success in any endeavor is based on many factors. We do not know your educational background, your skills, your prior experience, or the time you can and will devote to this course. Follow the advice of your personal advisors.

No guarantee is made that you will achieve any result at all from the ideas in our material. We will not share in your success, nor will we be responsible for your failure. The materials in our product and our course may contain information that includes or is based upon expectations or forecasts of future events. Any and all forward looking statements in our materials are intended to express our opinion of potential progress. They are opinions based on experiences only and should not be relied upon as hard facts for your success. Every person, experience, and individual is different.

Becoming A Published Author - Authors Course
ISBN# 13: 978-0-9887360-7-8
Copyright 2019 Dynasty's Visionary Publications. All Rights Reserved.

BECOMING A PUBLISHED AUTHOR

COURSE

Research

Writing Fiction

Volume #1 – Research Your Book

Do you dream of becoming the next bestselling author? Great! Then let's get started. Publishing a book can be exhilarating. Whether you want to write for a living or have a story you want to share with the world, following this course can get you there.

Please understand that being an author means you are running a business. You will wear many hats during this process such as; author, marketer, advertiser, researcher, speaker, accountant, bookkeeper, and many more. I'm not saying this to scare you. I'm saying it to prepare you for the awesome journey you are about to go on.

The first thing you will need to do is decide what type of book you want to write. Will it be Non-fiction or Fiction? It doesn't matter which one you choose. Both will require research. Yet, the research will be different for each. Unfortunately, this course is for those who want to become fiction authors. If becoming a fiction author is what you want, then you're in the right place.

Many people publish books to create an additional source of passive income or to make it a career. The choice is up to you. You might think that writing and publishing a book is a difficult process, but it's not. In fact, the journey to becoming a published author can be fun and enjoyable if you know what to do. Here's how to get started…

Determine the Audience of Your Book

Before you write a single word or start researching your topic, take some time to consider who you want to read your book. This is an important step, so don't skip it. Knowing who will be reading your work helps you to choose topics, find ideas, and research what's needed. You will need to take the time to reflect on what message you want your book to send to the reader and the type of audience that will purchase it.

Your book can also have more than one message. For example, you can write about Laura wanting to find real love (romance), but first she must gather the courage to leave her abusive husband (domestic violence). You now have two or more options to write about and it leaves room for you to introduce new characters which can lead to a book series. It's all up to you.

One thing to keep in mind when determining the overall audience of your book is to stay true to your message. Don't tell the reader the book is a romance, but when they read it, they find murder, gun play and other occurrences that they weren't interested in. This can lead to bad reviews.

You can also use a fiction book to build an email list. The same rule applies to fiction as it did to non-fiction. You can offer the book to readers for free and request their email so you can deliver the book digitally. Now you have their email address to send out a thank you note. Inside the note, make them aware that they will sometimes receive newsletters or future books from you. They will have the option to opt out. Most won't because they want to see if you will offer other free books. The upsell can be used here as well. You can offer your book or short story for free and present your newest release as an upsell.

Your book can also be used at speaking engagements depending on its genre. Domestic Violence, Child Abuse, Bully, and Cancer Survival are many books author's write to use at webinars and events. It can show your expertise about the subject or help the reader to relate to your story. Once your book is for sale, you can begin networking with other professionals and establish new contacts. It won't be long before you are quoted as a source and began receiving regular invitations to speak at various events.

Genre

A genre in literature represents a category or certain interest. Examples of genres are; Romance, Drama, Fantasy, Science Fiction, Westerns, Thriller, Mystery, Horror, and many more.

As an author you will need to decide which genre you will choose to write in. Do some research and see what others in your genre are writing. Check their writing technique, cover, information on the back cover, interior and audience response. Are they cross-selling other products like T-shirts or coffee mugs to their audience?

Knowing this information can help you shape your offer so that your audience responds favorably to your book. When you find authors who have built passive streams of income around their books, take the time to research them. Take notes on some of their ideas and make them your own. Tweak them to make them better. It's well worth the research and investment when your own book sales begin to rise.

Sources for Inspiration When Researching

It's not unusual to get stuck during the research phases of your book. This happens because you're new to this and have never done it before. But don't worry. It's not that hard to do. So let's get to it.

Now that you know what genre you want to write in, you need to come up with an idea for your book.

Let's say you want to write a love story about two people on vacation for two weeks and fall in love. They both live in different states and know they will need to leave to go back to their lives afterwards. So they enjoy the two weeks together, and when it's time to leave, things get emotional. However, after returning home she gets a call that the promotion she put in for was offered to her, but it requires her to relocate. She accepts and moves to a new state. Imagine her surprise when she walks in for her first day of work, and finds her vacation lover is her knew boss.

Now with this scenario, you will need to research vacation locations (hot or cold), the two states each character lives in, names for the character's, and so forth. Also, there will be other character's that will need names and duties, such as hotel staff and more. The best thing to do is write down all your ideas and keep them close. They will come in handy when it's time for you to create your outline. We will get more into that later.

With all the researching, there might come a time when you feel that you've exhausted all of your own ideas. Fortunately, you can refresh your ideas at any time. Here are a few techniques to help you with that.

Reading

A great way to get fresh ideas is to read other authors work. You don't do this to steal their ideas, but to see how well they've written their story. Was the book good? What made it good? Did it flow well? Check their scene development. Their character development. Maybe their main character had a speech impairment or a limp. This is done to make the character seem more real. You can learn a lot by reading other authors books, but make sure you're reading books that are in your genre. The more you immerse yourself in the work of other authors, the easier it becomes to make your own writing style stronger. That's because inspiration often multiplies. Sometimes, while you're still reading a book you will begin to get ideas. Once you've finished reading more ideas are likely to arrive soon after.

Google

When it comes to getting new ideas, **Google** is your best friend. You don't have to lean into meaty resources. Sometimes knowing what to add to your story is as simple as typing a phrase into the Google search bar. Whether its vacation spots, cars, sexy men, etc., Google has you covered. You can save links and return later to read up on what you've discovered. For example, I wanted a special spot for my hero to take my heroine, but I wanted something different. So I went to Google and typed in exclusive vacation spots. A lengthy list was provided and I clicked on quite a few links until I found the perfect spot. I then read up on the destination that I chose and jotted down some key details about it. I then added it to my story and just like that, my characters were playing on a secluded beach of bright white sand. It was that easy!

Videos

Videos can be another great source of inspiration when you're not sure what else to put in your story. One of the most popular and well-known video sites is **YouTube**. Type in your topic and search to see what comes up. If your story takes place in Mexico, type that in the search bar and see what pops up. People load their vacation videos, research video's etc., and you can watch them for free. You'll get to see what Mexico looks like in motion instead of glancing at still photos. To me, seeing it in real time is much better.

YouTube isn't the only video search engine you can use. There are also video sites like **Vimeo** where you can find a plethora of documentaries, vacation spots, and more.

Surveys

Dropping a question about the topic you're writing about is a great way to get information. It's even better knowing its coming from potential readers. Having their feedback shows you that it's something that they are interested in.

Relationship question about who's right or wrong are the best questions to ask. It gains the audience from both, men and women, and you'll see things heat up quickly. You can sit back and watch the free information roll in.

This doesn't have to be hard or technical. You can use a website like **SurveyMonkey** or **SurveyGizmo**. Create your survey by asking open-ended questions like: If you're a stay at home mom, and your husband pays all the bills, should he give you an allowance to spend on things you want? What are your thoughts?

Be sure to ask a question that will have your participants wanting to share what they've experienced. You never know what they'll say that might spark an idea or give you an insight to add to your book.

Once your survey is set up, send it out to your subscribers, blog readers, social media friends and anyone else in your community who's willing to take it. You may need to offer a small incentive to encourage people to click through your link and record their answers. This could be a small gift like a coupon code for one of your products, free a digital goodie like a short story ebook. Whatever you plan to offer, make sure your participants will value it enough to fill out your survey.

Social Groups

When it comes to getting new ideas, you don't have to lean into meaty resources. Sometimes knowing what to add to your outline is as simple as finding Facebook groups that cater to your audience. You can also join groups that cater to writing and authors. These are essential to gaining information on writing, free stuff and other things that can be of use to your writing journey. Not to mention, you might even meet one of your favorite authors!

You can do this by logging into Facebook and visiting their [groups page](). You will see a list of groups that you're already part of. However, if you look at the top, you'll also see a tab that reads "discover." Click that and you'll see a list of group suggestions.

The first list of group suggestions will be based on topics you've expressed interest in. But you'll also see local groups, groups that friends are in, and groups that are labeled hobbies and interests.

When you do find a few groups that seem like a good match, ask to join them. Some groups may have a questionnaire for you to fill out, so make sure that you do that. You should also look at the group rules to see if the group is a good match for you.

Once you're part of a few groups for your target audience and genre, spend some time browsing them. Ask questions from other members, and they will provide you with valuable information that you can use. Many times, these conversations can spark fresh inspiration and make you see your book in a whole new way.

Stay the Course

You might be tempted to skip the research. It may not seem as exciting or glamorous as some of the other steps involved. However, don't fall into this trap. Taking the time to do your research will help you write your book quickly and easily. It will also make the whole publishing process more enjoyable.

If you start to feel overwhelmed, give yourself permission to take a break. But don't give up. Come back to your book and keep working on it. When you have a published book in your hands, you'll feel so proud of yourself and be amazed at what you've accomplished.

Don't forget to check for your free templates and author information at the end of the course!

Volume #2 – Write Your Draft

Getting Creative

Now that you've chosen your genre, it's time to get creative. It's now time to write down all your ideas for the book. Don't worry about them being in any kind of order. That process will come later. Right now, you need to get down all you have on paper or typed in a document. Once you've written down your ideas, it's time to do more research and put those ideas in order. And the best way to do that is to start an outline. But before we have a completed outline, there are steps to follow. Let's get to it!

Step one: The overview

An overview is basically a brief description of what the book will be about.

Overview Example:

Sophie is relieved when the Powder Sugar Bakery is asked to bake a cake for a Spring Break party several states over. Surely trouble can't follow her this far? Sophie is proven wrong when three of the guests at the party drops dead unexpectedly, and she knows it's her job to figure out what's going on here – again. It seems that three friends of the party giver were poisoned by the cake, and as she begins questioning the guests and uncovering the truth, she finds out a whole host of despicable secrets. At this point, Sophie is beginning to think that someone on her team is responsible for the string of murders that are following her around, but she can't bring herself to focus on her betrayers, Lester and Serena. So Sophie buries herself in the crime, which becomes more and more mysterious as time goes on. Tensions mount as a fourth guest turns up dead, and she is racing against the clock to eliminate the killer before the killer eliminates her.

Problem and Solution

Now that you have a basic idea of what you want your book to be about, you can now start the brainstorming process by focusing on this question:

What is the problem you need to solve in the story?

After reading the overview I can tell exactly what Sophie's problem is. I can tell that she owns a bakery and has had trouble before with her customers dying. She now received another big job and at this job even more customers die. Now she believes its someone on her team sabotaging her company and she must do everything in her power to find out who and why, before someone else ends up dead. Or worse, her.

In your book you should have a problem that needs to be solved by your hero/heroine. Otherwise, you're not accomplishing anything in the book. Your book won't have any excitement and you'll be disappointed when it starts getting bad reviews.

After you have identified the problem in your story, it's now time to come up with a way to solve it. This process is called story development. Let me show you an easy way to develop your story into a first draft outline.

Story Development: Steps For A First Draft Outline

You will need a recorder. Since cell phones have them, let's use that. Open your recorder app and select the record button. Once it starts to record, this is the process you will use.

Imagine sitting across from your best friend. You're a witness to a crime (robbery), and you want to tell her everything you saw. I don't know about your friends, but mine would want to know every little detail, leaving nothing out. And now that you are the center of attention, you should want to hold their interest and have them hanging on your every word.

So you start to tell her what you saw from the beginning to the end. Don't start your story at the climax (when the crime happened). Start it from that morning when you first woke up and was upset that you had to cover another shift for an employee that always called out, yet never gets written up. Explain how you chose the perfect outfit, quickly shaved your legs, and sprayed on perfume because you liked the guy that worked in the cubicle next to yours. Make sure you list at breakfast you spilled coffee on your shirt and had to change it, which made you late.

Keep telling every detail not leaving anything out. Express how you felt. Did you see anything weird or funny? Did you smell the flowers as you walked past a garden. What did your breakfast taste like? Did you roll your eyes at a guy you use to date when he said hello to you in the hall? Tell everything that led up to the moment of the crime, then the crime itself, and lastly, what happened afterwards.

All these details are part of the story and will draw in the reader. They want to experience everything you did during that day. And if the details are exciting and juicy, they'll keep reading until the very end.

Dictation

Now that you've finished telling your friend everything that happened on the recorder, it's now time to dictate that recording and put it on paper. You will press play and write down every word you said. If you said something funny and your friend laughed, you write down that she laughed. If she sighed, you write down that too. If you said something sad, write down the emotion you see on her face. All of this is part of your story and will draw in the reader.

Once all of the recording has been dictated, you'll have your first draft.

Steps For The Second Draft

The second draft is where you embellish the story. You can add little details, change the settings, and be more creative with scene development. But here's where you really get to show your creativeness. Although you witnessed the crime (robbery), you don't know the details of why it was committed. So it's up to you to come up with a meaningful idea.

For example, you can say a guy worked at a jewelry store as a clerk and saw a flaw in the store's security. Maybe the guard was too old or had a habit of stepping outside to hit on women that passed by, leaving the store vulnerable. He passed this information on to his friends and they decided to rob the store thinking it would be an easy target. However, the moment they hit the store, inside was an off duty police officer who quickly dialed 911, and within moments the place was surrounded. Now you can embellish the story more with a hostage situation, or have the robbers try to escape. You have endless possibilities. Let your creativity flow.

Once you've added your creativeness to the whole story, go back in the draft and create character names, and add it to the story. You can use a detailed character sheet to keep all this new information handy. Trust me, it's easier to have this list to look at when you need an answer to a question. It beats scrolling back through the entire document to find your answer.

After going through your story and adding the new information and ideas, your second draft should be longer and flow even better. Based off your character sheet, you will have added supporting characters, a setting, added scenes and an ending.

You now have a second draft ready to be chapterized.

Chapterizing

Now that the second draft is ready, it's time to create chapters. Creating chapters are easy because the story draft is already done. Chapterizing is basically breaking down the story into scenes and placing that scene into a chapter. For example, if at the beginning of the story you are talking about getting dressed, spilling the coffee on your shirt and so forth, all that gets placed under Chapter 1.

Once you get to the office and have a run in with your boss, a co-worker, etc., the scene changes, which means it's a new chapter (Chapter 2). It will go on like that throughout your story. With every scene change (different place), it's a new chapter. And remember, all of this is already written out in your draft. By the time you get to the end of your draft, you should have a completed document filled with chapters. The best part about it is you still can go into the story, now that you see how it flows, and add little tidbits to make it even better.

Time To Write!

I know you're probably wondering 'Now What?' What do I do with these chapters? Well, once you read what you wrote under Chapter 1, you will see it's more like a brief summary of what takes place. At this time you began to write in detail about what happened. You're basically adding to what you already have. Check out the example below for a better understanding.

Chapter 1

Danielle turned over in bed and groaned angrily when she heard her alarm go off. It was Thursday, which usually was her day off, but she had been told to come in to cover for another employee. Kathy, called out at least three times a month and always seemed to dodge pink slips and keep her job. If that was me, I would have gotten the boot with the quickness, Danielle thought, pissed off as she lay there staring at the clock.

Watching the digital numbers click by slowly, she knew she had to get up and start getting ready. With an angry kick, she flung the blanket off her legs and slid to the side of the bed. "This sucks," she mumbled, as she stumbled sleepily towards the bathroom.

Do you see what I mean by writing out the story? You still have your draft summary telling you what goes on in the chapter. By the time you write everything out that is supposed to happen, you will have a full chapter written. Then you move on to chapter 2 and do the same. Once you do this for every chapter, you will have the first draft of a completed book.

Volume# 3 – Polish It

Writing a book is quite an accomplishment and you should be proud of yourself. Not many people reach the point where they can say they've written a book. But once you have completed the writing, the book is still not finished yet. There's more to do…

Make It Shine

Anyone who writes a book is often too emotionally invested to realize that it's not perfect as-is. If you're the only person who has read your book, then there's a 99.9% chance that you missed something that could impact the book's future success.

Since you only get one shot to make a good first impression, you don't want to disappoint your readers. If they are disappointed, the book may be marked as "DNF" (did not finish) by your audience.

Your book needs to appear professionally written or readers will move on quickly. For example, I rushed to publish my first book *'Loving Rainy Days: Volume 1 of The Tase Men Series'* before I took the time to make it the best it could be. I received a lot of criticism and negative reviews. Eventually, I took the book down and re-launched after it had been edited and with a new cover. I immediately saw major improvements and started receiving Five Star reviews.

When it comes to polishing your book, you need to set aside time to read it cover to cover in one sitting. There's a lot of advice that tells writers to "let the book sit" but this isn't a good thing to do. You want to re-read the book while it's fresh in your mind. Otherwise, you might forget something important.

As you read your book again, don't read it from an editing mindset. Instead, look at it through the eyes of a reader. See if you can answer exactly what it's about within the first few pages. If your message isn't clear, you run the risk of losing your audience's interest and they'll put your book down.

When you go back to the beginning to polish your book, you want to make sure that it opens with a hook. A hook is a sentence or two that's compelling, interesting, and lures in readers. Your opening hook is what makes your audience want to keep turning the pages.

As you read your book, notice the flow of your content. Do you hop from one topic to another in a way that's not coherent? Does your thoughts flow clearly or is it easy to lose your place due to confusion? Following your outline can be helpful. It will act as a readability checklist. By following it, you can see if you covered each thought or topic and ensure your thoughts are flowing smoothly. Books that are easy to read have a higher readability quotient. They're also more pleasant for readers and because of that, they're more likely to review your book and recommend it to others.

The 3 Stages of Editing

The hardest work you'll ever do to your book is the editing. You may think of editing as merely checking the grammar and spelling or looking for typos. While it's true that these are editing tasks, they aren't the whole process.

A thorough edit involves three separate stages. Your book isn't ready for publication until you've completed these edits, and even then, you may find yourself needing to revisit an editing stage. If you feel that you aren't cut out for the editing process, or don't have the time, then you should definitely hire someone else to take up the project. This means someone professional. Not a family member that always got good grades. The editing process is too important for slacking.

Stage #1: Developmental Editing

The first stage of editing is what's known as developmental editing. During this phase, you read through your entire book and you make notes as you go. Start by looking for inconsistencies.

As you read your book, pay attention to the overall tone of your book. If you're sharing a story about someone else, make sure that you don't accidentally give the person the wrong name or title. Little details like this can distract your audience and make reading your book less enjoyable for them. Also during this stage, you'll want to double check your character descriptions, settings or facts that you mention for accuracy. You can do this by reverting back to your outline draft or Character Sheet.

It's essential that you examine whether each chapter has a strong enough hook or action point to carry it. If you fizzled out of ideas for the chapter and tried to pad the word count with useless information, you need to go back and rewrite it or remove it. It's okay to have a short chapter.

In developmental editing, you're checking for anything that would jar your reader out of what you're saying and fix it. You want to make sure that you tap into the emotions of your audience. Readers who relate to the emotions you mention are more likely to be moved by what they are reading. It will make them connect with the characters and be anxious for more.

Books that motivate, inspire, make them laugh, misty or touch them on a personal level, are ones that an audience will not only remember, but will gladly share with others. It's the easiest way to get word of mouth marketing.

Finally, you need to edit the content for your voice and personality. Your voice is made up of your life experiences, your beliefs, and your attitudes. You want that to shine through. It's what makes your book unique. In other words, your "secret sauce" keeps readers turning the pages.

Remember, the best books aren't the ones created by experts or niche leaders. The best ones are written from the heart of a writer trying to connect with their audience. So if your book doesn't sound like you wrote it, rework it until it does.

Stage #2: Line Editing

The second stage of editing is known as line editing. Some writers confuse this stage with proofreading since proofreading and editing is often used in place of each other, but that's not what this is.

Proofreading focuses on surface mistakes like typos. Line editing focuses on how you've written your story and making sure it flows smoothly. It's the phase where you check to make sure you've written your ideas in the best possible way. Here is where you'll push yourself to go deeper into the book and make it the strongest it can be.

Start by looking for places where you've said the same thing. You may have repeated yourself, but just worded it differently.

At this point in the editing process, you'll look for paragraphs that need tightening. If your wording makes it hard to understand or may confuse the reader, you need to rewrite that paragraph or section.

Long, unbroken, descriptive paragraphs or an overwhelming amount of detail (known as fluff), slows the pacing. Look for paragraphs that are difficult to read because there are too many words such as run on sentences. You will need to shorten them. If a detail isn't important to the chapter or story, consider cutting it. Be willing to let go of words that don't strengthen your book.

You should also cut portions that don't tie in with the main theme. Paragraphs that veer off topic or thoughts that don't serve a purpose should be removed. Remember, every time you cut something from your book, you're trying to make it stronger.

It might be tempting to use big, complicated words in an effort to impress your audience. However, you have to keep in mind that not every reader is on the same level. Keep your book simple so that it will be appealing to everyone. Also, try to refrain from using slang terms that are only available to you, or your neighborhood. Other's may not know the meaning of those terms and may leave the reader frustrated and ready to toss your book aside.

Reading your work out loud to see how it sounds is a great way to hear the flow. If you find yourself having to re-reading a sentence or paragraph, then the phasing is probably awkward and needs to be tightened. As you read through each paragraph, check to see what the reader will experience from it and I there were enough details to keep them reading.

While line editing, look for "pet" words. Every writer has them—they're the words that slip into your book seemingly on their own. Commonly overused words include:

- Just
- Only
- Really
- Totally
- Completely
- Somewhat
- Somehow
- Absolutely
- Basically
- Actually
- Sort Of
- Pretty
- Very
- Kind Of
- Yeah
- Okay
- Said

Often the words above just weaken your sentences. They water down your meaning and can even confuse readers depending on how you use them. Keep in mind that line editing is all about the flow of your words and how they sound together. Don't be afraid to experiment and rewrite sentences if you can make them stronger.

Stage #3: Copyediting

The final stage of editing is known as copyediting. In this phase, you'll look for common grammatical errors. Even if you're great at grammar, you don't want to skip this step. It can be easy to accidentally switch words. For example, you used *farther* when you meant *further*.

Other words that are easily confused or switched up during the writing process include:

- Accept/Except
- Affect/Effect
- It's/Its

- You're/Your
- Illicit/Elicit
- Pour/Pore
- Advice/Advise
- Ensure/Insure
- Aloud/Allowed
- Principle/Principal
- Site/Sight
- There/Their

As you're editing in this stage, make sure your verbs agree with your tense. You'll also want to check to make sure you didn't accidentally use a homonym incorrectly. Homonyms are words which sound alike or are spelled alike, but have different meanings. For example: Robert used "bare" (nude), when he meant "bear" (animal), in his book. These simple mistakes can change the whole meaning of your sentence and confuse your readers.

If you're using an office program, it's easy to find the number of times you used a repetitive word. Press Ctrl + H and that will bring up a dialog box. Type in the word you'd like to check in the *'Find What'* section and it'll show you how often you used the word.

Besides switching words, misspellings are also something you'll want to watch for. While most writing programs will catch commonly misspelled words, some won't—especially if the words are unusual such as slang.

When you reach the copyediting phase, this is your last chance to make sure that everything in your book is as polished as it can be. So now is the time to double-check your dates, character names, descriptions, settings and other important information.

During copyedits, you should listen to your manuscript. Hearing the words out loud will help you determine if the sentences read smoothly or if they are jarring. Most devices have a feature known as "Screen Reader". PC users can find this feature under "Windows Accessories." Turn on the screen reader and pull up your document. Let the program read your words back to you. This will help you see if you are transitioning smoothly when introducing new scenes and thoughts.

Since copyediting is the final stage of editing, study your punctuation and keep an eye out for mistakes. These mistakes can include things like forgetting to put something in quotation marks or having a period at the end of a sentence that needs a question mark instead. Check for too many spaces in between words and sentences.

Remember, the point of copyediting is to present your content in a way that's coherent without confusing or overwhelming your readers. You want your words to be invisible, so your story can play in their mind like a movie.

Finding Beta Readers

Now that you've completed the editing stages of your book, you're ready to take the next step. This involves finding other people to read over it before the book is published.

The purpose of doing this is so that you can receive feedback on what you've written. When you use beta readers, you end up with a quality, refined book because others will often catch what you've missed.

Think of your beta readers as your test group. These readers will help you eliminate problems before the book goes live. They can see your book and its flaws more clearly because they aren't as close to the content as you are. You'll also discover if your book is right for your target audience. If your audience has questions or doubts, you'll be able to tweak the book using their input. Another upside to using beta readers is that you can have them do pre-reviews of your book before it comes out.

These pre-reviews will go up on their social media profiles or book websites. This creates a buzz for your book before it's released. Then, these reviews can be added to your platform's author page so that when the book is published, you already have plenty of positive reviews.

Finding beta readers won't be difficult if you have a decent following already. You can send out the call for beta readers to your email list. Alternatively, you can put a notice up on your website or social media page, letting your followers know you're looking for someone to read the finished product before it goes on sale. If you do not have a large following, you can still put the announcement out across your social media. However, you can also reach out in forums or groups that you belong to asking for beta readers.

Finding beta readers is easier if you look in communities where you're known. That's because joining a group just to find beta readers isn't very effective. If no one knows who you are, chances are they won't care about your book. One thing you can do is connect with an author who writes in the same genre. You can ask them if they'll put a "shout out" on social media for you. Another option would be to ask if they're interested in bartering or participating in a book swap option.

Some people might advise you to send out your book to family members or to your friends. This is not always a good idea. They can check for grammar and mistakes, but if they're not your target audience, you don't really get a good feel for whether or not your book works. Your family and friends may also be more hesitant to tell you the truth about your book. In the interest of not wanting to hurt your feelings, they might simply say that they liked or enjoyed it, which doesn't help you polish your book. You need people who will be honest with you because they don't have anything at stake.

Keep in mind that you should ask more people than you think you'll need because inevitably, someone won't come through and finish reading the book before launch time.

To make sure the beta reader experience is a good one for you and them, they need some guidance. Email the reader the book along with a checklist or set of instructions. Include a date that you need their responses back to you. Give yourself plenty of time to make any changes beta readers suggest before you go live.

In your instructions, ask the reader to write down the page number and anything on that page that needs your attention. This might be a grammar mistake or a typo. It could be something they didn't understand, or something they feel was explained in too much detail.

Specifically ask if your words resonated with them. In addition, find out if what you said made sense to them, held their attention, related to them, and what their overall feel for the story was as they read. When the halfway point has passed for when the feedback is due, send out a reminder email along with a message saying you hope they're enjoying your book.

When you receive your feedback, some of it will be helpful, but some of it won't be. You have to separate the comments that point out a legitimate problem from the ones that want to rewrite your passages based on opinion. Not every beta reader will be as informed as you about the story's subject matter, so their comments may not always be valid.

If you receive enthusiastic responses from the beta readers, select a few of them to contact and tell them you're going to highlight portions of their comments and put them under editorial reviews. Be sure to keep a list of every beta reader, who completely read your book and turned it into you with notes. You'll want to be sure and thank these people in the acknowledgement section, so they know you appreciate their hard work. You can also use these same readers for your next book.

Tools to Help You Edit & Polish Your Book

When you're editing your book, you may need help organizing all your thoughts, ideas, images, charts, and other information. For that, you can use Scrivener. You can [see the screenshots here](#).

The program allows you to work on your book one chapter at a time with the ability to rearrange your thoughts or sections of the chapter easily. You can leave notes to yourself within the application and you can also add things like tables or images. The software is also compatible with audio files.

You may also want to get a program that can help you with spelling because there's no doubt that you're going to make mistakes as you write your book. However, these mistakes can be caught if you use the right tools to help you polish your book. Some writers swear by using the spellcheck feature in their writing program. But these spellchecks aren't always reliable. They often can't tell the difference between a word that sounds similar to the one you actually meant to use.

For example, you might mistakenly write: *The software isn't affective for the job*. What you mean to write was: *The software isn't effective for the job*.

The second sentence uses the correct word effective, but spellcheck wouldn't catch the mistake and correct it for you. Therefore, you would unintentionally change the meaning of your sentence if you only rely on spellcheck. You don't have to carry the burden of editing alone. There are plenty of online tools that you can use. Some of these are paid resources, but others are free or have special trials you can take advantage of.

One of the best sites for editing your book is **Grammarly**. It has both a free and premium edition that you can use, including a browser button you can insert to check your spelling and grammar when you're writing emails or posting to social media. However, you can also use it for any of your writing projects, including the ones that are book length. Not only will the resource point out spelling errors, but it will also perform a basic check of your writing.

If you need more help finding problems like vocabulary errors, grammatical mistakes, and punctuation, then you would choose the paid premium option. In addition, the software will check to make sure your words are concise and tell you why you should change the parts that are flagged as needing to be rewritten. Then it will give you a suggestion on how to fix the issue.

Besides Grammarly, you might also like, **Pro Writing Aid**. This software also has both a free and a paid edition. In the free edition, the program will only check about 500 words at a time (that's roughly one page of content). However, with the paid version, you can upload your entire book and have it checked.

One of the features that users like best about Pro Writing Aid is that it offers "writing reports." With these, the program will look over what you submit to determine how to make it better. It will check for style, grammar, words that you overuse, sentence lengths, transitions and more. Not only will this improve your current book, it will help you become aware of your writing weaknesses so you can improve other content you write like blog posts, short reports, and more.

You can also use the **Online Grammar Check** from SEO Magnifier. It checks your writing for spelling and grammatical errors. It also searches your sentences to ensure they have the proper subject/verb agreement. Since you can only upload small files at a time, this site is best used for people who want to turn their previously written articles or blog posts into a book.

If you're looking for a proofreading website, try [Language Tool](#). It highlights errors and recommends alternative solutions. The exciting thing about Language Tool is that it can differentiate between English based on the dialectic you choose. For example, you can use the tool to check your content and note problems in American English, Canadian English, and others.

You can use the free version of the tool to check up to 20,000 characters (that's roughly 4,000 words). Therefore, you could presumably use it to check your book chapter by chapter if you wanted to stick with the free version. If you'd rather do all of your book at once or if you want additional features, they have an affordable monthly option that might be a good fit for you.

Don't Rush It

In the excitement of having your book completed, it's natural to want to begin working on the publishing process. You're proud of your new book and you want to share it with the world. However, it's important that you take the time to slow down and polish your creation. You don't want to release a second-rate book that taints your reputation and turns off potential readers from your brand.

Instead, be patient during this time. Remember that your goal isn't just to publish a good book. Your goal is to create an outstanding novel that readers can proudly recommend. That means giving yourself the space and time to rework your book. When you're done, you'll have a finished product that you can proudly promote to your audience, knowing it will inspire and delight them for years to come.

BECOMING A PUBLISHED AUTHOR
AUTHORS COURSE

Publishing

Volume# 4 – Publishing Your Book

Once your book is written and edited, it's time to start the publishing phase. During this final stage, you'll focus on the formatting and the process of uploading your book to the various publishing platforms and/or making it available on your website.

Creating the Back Cover Information

The first thing you should focus on in writing the back cover information is the synopsis. The synopsis is a brief description of your book. When writing the synopsis, you must do so with just a few words due to space constraints. The standard amount of words is around 200 or less. This means you have to make sure you use clear and persuasive phrases so potential readers will want to buy your book.

Don't get too wordy on the back of your book. When readers are considering what to buy, they look at the synopsis. If that's too long, they'll skim your words and could miss important details. The back of your book should offer a peek at what's inside, but the main purpose of the synopsis is to work as your advertisement.

While writing the synopsis of your book might seem easy, it's often one of the most difficult parts of finishing up. The reason for this is because you have to condense the main points, purpose, and theme of your book in just a paragraph or two.

How you format the back cover information is entirely up to you. But do keep in mind that it should be written in a way that allows for easy reading and holds the attention of the reader to the very end. You can begin the synopsis using several different styles. One of these is by starting with a question.

For example, *"Have you ever loved someone so hard that you lost yourself in the process?"*

With this question you've stated a problem in your book. Right away the reader can see that the character in this book is struggling some kind of way. They will want to continue to read to find out the problem the character is facing.

At this point you will introduce your character by name (Stacy). Explain Stacy's dilemma and how she got there. Then add a hardship that is holding her back from getting through it.

Next, you will introduce a second character (Mike). Mike could be the reason why Stacy is in the hardship and keeping her from getting over it, and moving on. Explain what he's doing to hold her back.

Finally, you want to produce some more questions to hook the reader.

Example, *Will Stacy leave Mike once the truth is finally revealed? Will she once again give in to his charm and stay stuck in a loveless marriage? Or will the pain be too much for her to forgive?*

You now have a synopsis that will draw in the reader. They now want to know what the big secret is and if Stacy will stay or leave. It sounds pretty cut and dry, but remember, you will have a full novel with twist and turns that will hypnotize the reader until the very end.

Another tidbit to add to the back cover is a blurb or quote. A blurb can be written by a fellow author, a reader, or anyone that is affiliated in the same genre. Getting a quote from your friend or relative is okay too, as long as they have read the book to offer a statement relevant to the story. The best thing to do is to get a quote from someone that your audience would recognize when they see the name. You will gain readership based off the trust of their readers and their notoriety.

A short author bio is a great way to introduce yourself to readers. It's basically a brief look at how you arrived where you are in your life. You might mention who you are and why you decided become a writer. You can also add your education, your accomplishments, etc., if it's relevant to the book. You want to be careful that you don't come across as bragging. If you write in an arrogant tone, it can turn away readers.

All in all, just keep in mind that if your synopsis and bio doesn't create a need in the reader to want to read it, then they won't feel the urge to buy it.

Write Your Amazon Description

Let's face it, Amazon is the 'go to' place to self-publish your book. One of the most important parts of listing your book on Amazon is the description (synopsis). Creating the description of your book is pretty easy. The reason for this is because you can pull what you wrote as the synopsis on the back cover and use it directly in the description.

You want to add to your description by creating a headline that will grab the attention of your readers. This hook is used for the purpose of capturing attention so that they'll read the rest of the description. You need this headline to be as intriguing or as eye-catching as possible because Amazon doesn't display the entire description at first. They show a small portion, and you will need to click on 'read more' to read the whole synopsis.

All you have to *wow* the audience with is whatever you've written above their fold. This means you must reach your audience first with a short phrase or one sentence headline. The next few sentences that you write after that (your synopsis), will have to speak to the reader in a way that tells them what your book is about.

Depending on the way Amazon formats the "read more" area of your book, you will only have between two and five sentences to 'wow' the audience and convince them to buy your book. You want to give enough away here to summarize the book, but not so much that the reader feels you've shared everything, and now don't need to buy the book.

One way that you can check to make sure your book description looks good is to do a market check. Do this by pulling up books within your genre that touch on a topic like the one you've written about. Study how those descriptions were written and that will help you get a hint as to whether you're in the range of what's hot and trending. Keep in mind that you only want to study books that are ranking well on the site.

There is a limit to how much you can say within your book description. Amazon will cut off the words, even mid-sentence, if you go over the space parameters of what they allow. That means you get roughly between 400-500 words.

It can be easy to go over that limit if you try to include your biography within your description. Don't do that. Save the "about you" information for lower on the page under your author section. Sometimes writers try to cram everything in the description because they think the audience won't scroll below the line to find out more information, but that's not true.

Your audience will almost always scroll down the page to see what others are saying about the book which is a good reason why you want to have reviews lined up before your book goes live on the site.

Build Your "Author Central" Page

Every publishing platform has an "Author Central" page. This page typically features a picture of the author, the writer's biography, and links to the author's books, website and social media profiles. There's a lot you can do with your author page that can tell the audience about you, but it can also be used to help you promote and sell your book. Don't miss the opportunities that are available for you in this section that Amazon and other publishers give you.

Start by making sure that you have a good author image ready to upload. This can be a professional photo, but it doesn't have to be since the purpose is to connect a face with the book. A photo builds audience trust, so you can use a high-resolution selfie that looks nice as long as the photo is good quality.

In your biography section, you can copy the same bio from the back cover of your book. You want the audience to see your bio and know that you are open to sharing small tidbits of your life and that they can trust you to present them with quality written work.

Some authors try and write clever or cute bios where they talk about their pets or hobbies. These are not a waste of space, but be sure to not give out too much of your private life. Keep your safety first at all times.

Bios should always be written in the third person. It's the standard format, but there's a good reason to write it in the third person. It sounds more professional and less like you're bragging on yourself or boasting about the success you've had.

Third person example: *Kim Dexter is the author of several books. She has been writing since grade school and now has over 20 books in her catalog.*

One question that inevitably comes up on concerning the about the author page is how long your bio should be. The answer is that it should be easily digestible by the reader. No more than about a paragraph and you want to keep the tone personal or conversational in nature.

It can be helpful to use this format when writing your bio:

1. Open with a sentence that's memorable or stirs an emotion with the reader.
2. Mention who you are and why you're an author.
3. Showcase your ability or talents, but be humble about it.
4. Read other books by (Author Name)
5. Contact information

Something many writers forget is that the end of their bio is another chance to create a promotional opportunity. Never end your bio with a sentence that wraps everything up. You always want to have an open ending. You know, that "wait, there's more" ending. That means you should finish off your bio with an incentive.

Urge your reader to look at other books in your series or supporting material such as your podcasts or video. If you don't have any of that, then encourage readers to follow you on social media. You always want to leave the reader with the ability to learn more about you, or from you, in order to build a relationship that can turn into a conversion.

The Amazon author page is also, where you can add early reviews of your books. To do this, you would sign in to your page, locate your book from the list if you have more than one and click on the book. Once you do that, you'll have the option to add the reviews to the different formats. Select the format.

You'll then be presented with a box that gives you several options. Choose "Review" and when you do that, a box will open for you to paste the reviews in. You want to bold certain words or phrases within the reviews that highlight your book. These would be things like "well-written" or "best book I've read." Any words that can boost interest or promotion for your book is what you want to bold.

Once you have the reviews you want to include on your author page, then click preview to make sure the bold remained and all the punctuation stayed the same. If it didn't just go back and fix it, then preview again. Don't worry. Amazon's uploader is a little tricky so you may have to work with the formatting several times before it saves correctly.

Design Your Book Cover

When you're ready for your book's cover, you can create it yourself, use an online cover creator tool, or hire someone else to create it for you. If you use Amazon, they have something called "Cover Creator" that will walk you through each step to create your own cover. The software will show you some sample covers so you can see if you like that style before you make the decision to use it.

Kindle Publishing uses stock images, which is standard, even among cover designers. You can choose to use a stock image that you've purchased or have a license to use. If you choose to do it yourself, be aware that Amazon has qualifications before a cover is accepted. Your cover will be rejected if the display image isn't correct.

This usually happens when you're not familiar with settings and margins that need to be followed in order to correctly create or upload the image. It can cause the image to be distorted. Any images that are blurry or controversial won't be accepted as covers. If you use any kind of promotional material on the cover, such as images featuring brands, logos or you have the word free, Amazon will reject the cover.

After you've selected your design, you'll pick the colors and fonts. Then you'll have the chance to look over the cover before you publish. Watch out for titles or author names that aren't easily readable, or characters that look like they were cut and pasted into the picture. If you can see the edges of the images, they're not blended seamlessly like they should be. This can sometimes happen when you use an image that you didn't crop correctly.

Once you preview your book cover and everything looks good, then you're ready to upload it. If you don't want to use Amazon's tool, there are paid ebook cover resources that you can choose from. Some of the sites will require you to create an account or sign in using Facebook or a Google account.

A great place for having a cover designed is at **Dynasty's Visionary Designs**. Dynasty's Visionary Designs assist authors that are working with a tight budget. They have reasonable prices and give quality design work. You can choose from a pre-made design or have one custom made for the same low price. They also offer promotional designs such as posters, business cards, banners and more. The great thing about this company is that they take all the frustration and guess work out of loading your cover. They resize it according to Amazons specs and email the files to you in PDF format, ready for loading (Amazon Print, KDP, Barnes and Noble, Smashwords, Draft2Digital, iBooks and more).

Another site to purchase cover designs is **[Self Pub Book Covers](#)**. If you're looking for inexpensive, pre-made book covers, you've found another great resource on the web for self-publishing authors. They also offer print designs at an extra cost.

You can buy your own stock images to have your book cover designed or you can work with a designer who will find the images for you. Many designers have different options and prices when it comes to book design. What you want to check for is that you'll get commercial use rights and/or the source file. If you get the source file, you're free to edit or change the design, as well as have another designer work on it. Many designers charge a fee for you to receive the source file. This is mainly because once you make changes, they won't go back into the file to correct any mistakes you make.

You also want to pay attention to revision limits. Look for designers that offer unlimited revisions or at least more than one or two. You also want to check out the designers reviews. Ask some of their customers how their experience was working with them. If they have a lot of positive feedback, then you're most likely in good hands.

Another option is to find a designer on **[UpWork](#)**. In their search bar, type in book cover or book cover design and you'll get a list of options. The designers will be listed by area of expertise, as well as the amount of work they've done and their charges for a project.

The cool thing about UpWork is that you can speak to various designers until you find one that you're comfortable with. Try to pick a designer who has made covers for books in your genre. This will ensure you choose someone who understands your vision and the vibe you're going for. Keep in mind that some designers' prices may exceed your budget. So be prepared to keep searching.

Format Your Book for Kindle

If you don't understand how to format your book for Kindle or Print, then you need to outsource this task. Otherwise, you'll end up with orphan words or long, unbroken paragraphs and sentences that are split in weird places. You could even end up with your Table of Contents combining with your first chapter. Half of the content might appear on one page and the rest of it on another. It's a nightmare to sort it and better to leave to a professional.

If you plan to use Kindle Direct Publishing, **[Amazon has a guide](#)** that will walk you through the process step-by-step. You want to make sure that your manuscript is stripped of any formatting that will cause issues when you upload it. That means if you used bold, indented chapters or italicized some words, you'll need to revert the manuscript back to the normal appearance.

Highlight your text and click on *Normal* to get your manuscript cleaned up from any previous formatting. If your manuscript was saved as a DOCX, you'll have to re-save it as a DOC since the platform doesn't convert DOCX.

Make sure that your indentions and spaces are in Kindle format style. The first line must be at 0.2" and make sure that your line spacing is set to single. All chapter titles should be on "center" using "Heading 1." Wherever you end one of your pages, you need insert "page break". If you don't, your chapters will run together.

If you do have images that need to be added, the best way to put those in your upload is by selecting Kindle Create, otherwise, the sizing could be messy. You'll also use Kindle Create to make your Table of Contents.

Review and Make Any Corrections

After your book is written and ready to be uploaded, you need to check to make sure that you've covered all the information concerning your book. Go over this carefully because you want your book in the right area where it'll have the chance to get to the correct audience.

First, check the genre that your book is listed under to make sure that it's correct. Then look at the categories. The reason that you want to be sure the categories are correct is because putting your book in the right category can make the difference between selling a few books and selling a lot of books.

It's easy to figure that the more books you sell, the better odds you have of hitting an Amazon list. However, putting your book in a category means it's competing against all the other books in that category. You can help your book sell well by choosing categories based on the genre. The more you narrow down your book categories, the higher your ranking will be.

So if you have a book on yoga, you would choose categories Health, Fitness & Dieting, then you would also select Exercise & Fitness. From there, you would break those categories down further by categorizing the book as Fitness. Many authors stop there and don't continue to break the book down into more categories, which is a mistake. What you want to do is keep looking. Find categories where the #1 Amazon best sellers are ranking with higher numbers of books sold in that category.

For example, when you click on yoga, it brings up a list of possible related words in more specific categories like; ab workouts, aerobics for children, for the aging, hip & thigh workouts and more. You would want to check each of those categories to see what the rankings were for the books that were #1 best sellers.

Choose the category related to your book where the best sellers had to be something like 10,000 or more. That means you have to sell less books per day to hit a list. It could mean the difference between selling 10 books in a day versus needing to sell over 700 in a day. You want to choose a category this way because it means more exposure for your book. The books that hit Amazon's list are heavily featured and promoted.

Amazon tags are small boxes that feature phrases or words that are pulled from your reviews. For a yoga book, this might be something like yoga poses or yoga practice. However, tagging can also pull praise tags such as beautifully written or wonderful book.

Publish

Finally, when all the work is done, you've checked the book for mistakes and placed it in the correct categories, it's time to hit the publish button. It may take a few hours or days before your book goes live. So when you're preparing your launch date, keep that in mind. You don't have any control over when Amazon will upload the book to the platform.

Once the book is live, you can check the formatting and see if there are any mistakes. If so, you can re-upload the book after the issue is corrected. When you're sure that everything is good, congratulate yourself. You've written and published a book and that's quite an amazing feat. You deserve the applause!

Don't forget to check for your free templates and author information ON THE NEXT PAGE!

FREE GOODIES TEMPLATES AND INFORMATION

get to know
YOUR CHARACTER'S APPEARANCE

- the basics -
approximate height, build, weight, coloring, age, gender, ethnicity, and identifying features

- the lifestyle -
their profession, their hobbies, their habits

- the faults -
the things that keep them from being gods among men

- the clothes -
what they wear in the workplace, running errands, at a party, and at home

- the body language -
eye contact, gait, carriage, posture, proximity, hand movements, and nervous ticks

INCREASE YOUR STORY'S TENSION

Tension: The anticipation of what will happen next in a story.

1. Don't let your characters have what they want.

2. Ask how you can make your character's situation worse.

3. Build flaws and conflict into your setting/story world.

4. Create conflict between your characters.

5. Increase the consequences of failure for the hero.

CHANGE PARAGRAPHS WHEN...

A NEW CHARACTER COMES ALONG

A NEW EVENT HAPPENS

A NEW IDEA IS INTRODUCED

THE SETTING CHANGES

A NEW PERSON IS SPEAKING

TIMES MOVES FORWARD OR BACKWARD

THE POINT OF THOUGHT MOVES TO ANOTHER PERSON

WORD PROCESSORS TO USE

Using word processors is the smartest and easiest way to get your project done. I know some people still write their book out by hand first I did with my first book Loving Rainy Days), then type it up afterwards. But basically, going digitally first makes a lot more sense. Once you're done, it makes the proofreading and editing that much easier.

[Microsoft Word](#) is still the greatest word processor out there. It's the most used software for editing jobs because of its great features and awesome free templates.

[Google Docs](#) is great for short and long projects. You will need an excellent internet connection, because if it goes down and you haven't saved your document, then say bye to all of your hard work.

[Scrivener](#) is a word-processing program and book outliner designed for authors. It provides an organizational system for documents, and notes. You will be able to organize notes, ideas, research and whole documents for easy access and reference.

[Pro Writing Aid](#) is also awesome for authors. Their software offers a grammar checker, style editing, and a writing mentor in one package. Whatever your genre of writing, Pro Writing Aid will assist you in achieving your goals.

Tip: When you're writing and you find yourself repeatedly using the same words, turn to a thesaurus for help. Here's the online thesaurus that I use. It's free!

[Thesaurus.com](#)

PUBLISHING YOUR BOOK

This is to help you with uploading your ebook and Paperback book to Kindle Direct Publishing (KDP).

After you have finished writing your book, take the time to go through the steps below before you upload to Amazon, or any other platform.

EDITING - Hire a professional to do this.
You can join a few writing groups and put up a post asking for reputable editors. Ask for references, pricing, and how quick is the turn around. Also, reach out to a couple of their clients to ask questions about their business process to make sure they are a good fit for your needs.

BOOK INTERIOR CHECK
Add whatever you see fit into the interior of your book to reach your readers and to make it stand out. Below is a list of common things authors add to their books.

Title Page
Copyright
Dedication
Acknowledgement
Contact Information
About The Author
Thank You Note
Table of Contents

FORMATTING - Hire a professional to do this.
Dynasty Visionary Designs offers great help to self-publishing authors. To format your book, they only charge $40. Inbox them to ask more about this great service.
www.facebook.com/dynastys.coverme

COVER DESIGN (Ebook and Print)
For a great cover design check out Dynasty Visionary Designs. They have awesome prices, great customer service, and a quick turnaround. They also will add your synopsis, resize the cover according to Amazon's requirements, and issue you a PDF in Press Quality.
www.facebook.com/dynastys.coverme

Once the main factors of your book are completed, you will also need the following information. Get everything together so the loading process will go smoothly and without a hitch.

Title (As it is on the cover)

Series (Only if your book is part of a series)

Subtitle (If you have one)

Author (Your name and any contributing authors)

Contributors (Editor, Illustrator, etc.)

Description/Synopsis
This should be the same as it is on the cover, however, you can add a call to action before you add the synopsis.

ISBN# (Print Books Only)
An ISBN is required for print books. KDP provides a free ISBN to publish your paperback. You can also buy your own ISBN from **Bowker.com** or through your local ISBN agency.

Keywords (7 keywords relating to your book)

Category/Genre (Amazon allows you to choose 2)

Language (English for US)

Publishing Rights: Go to **Copyright.com** to protect your work against plagiarism. The price for copyrighting is $35.00.

Age and grade range (optional)

Retail Price (What you charge and the royalties you will receive)
With Ebook royalties, you can choose between the 35% royalty option and the 70% royalty option. Paperback royalties offers a fixed 60% royalty rate sold on Amazon marketplaces and KDP will support paperback distribution for your book. KDP will pay you royalties from your book every month. That is roughly 60 days after the end of the month in which they were netted.

Pre-order (Optional)

Tip: In order to get your royalties paid to you from Amazon, you will need a bank account. However, if you don't have a bank account, here are 3 other methods to use instead.

1. **Rush Card** – When you set up a rush card account, they will offer you direct deposit by showing you a virtual blank check with the bank's name, router number, and your account number on it. This is all the information you need to load to Amazon to start receiving your royalties.

2. **Green Dot Card** - When you set up a Green Dot account, they will offer you direct deposit by showing you a virtual blank check with the bank's name, router number, and your account number on it. This is all the information you need to load to Amazon to start receiving your royalties.

Marketing Your eBook Checklist

Publishing your eBook is only half the battle. Now you need to get the word out about it so readers can find and buy it. Here's what to do:

Promote Your Book Through Your Website

- ☐ **Put an excerpt on your website.** Have the first chapter up for your audience to read. At the end of the excerpt, feature a call-to-action button or buy links.

- ☐ **Have a dedicated page for your book.** Put up the cover, the testimonials and all the buy links. If you don't have any testimonials, then use sentences from your book but make them tweetable.

- ☐ **Blog on relevant topics.** Write blog posts about the same subject but not as in-depth. Then tell readers that for more help, they can get the book.

- ☐ **Create a media page with all of your book information.** Make it easy for podcast hosts and journalists to interview you or feature your book.

Get Social With It

- ☐ **Put the book on your LinkedIn profile.** List it under your job experience as "author of (your book's title)". You can also mention the book in your LinkedIn groups if a relevant discussion comes up.

- ☐ **Promote your book on Twitter by doing a giveaway.** Use hashtags like #giveaway #contest #(authorname)win.

- ☐ **Create a branded hashtag for your book.** Include this hashtag whenever you're posting about your book and encourage your reviewers to do the same.

- ☐ **Be sure to add the book to your author page.** In addition to adding it to the information section, create a banner with your book cover on it.

- ☐ **Create a Facebook launch event.** Invite your social media followers to attend and encourage them to post about it on their profile.

- ☐ **Make a book trailer for your book.** This doesn't have to be long—think 30-60 seconds. Just long enough to tease your readers and make them curious enough to click.

Harness the Power of Email Marketing to Sell Your Book

- ☐ **Tease your subscribers.** Let your list know a project you've been working on is about to be released but don't tell them what it is.

- ☐ **Send a sneak peek.** This should be a glance at the cover or a short excerpt that's shared only with your list.

- ☐ **Do a final reveal.** Proudly show off your new book to your subscribers. Let them know where they can pick up a copy.

- ☐ **Offer a freebie.** Give your list related promotional material such as an exclusive video or podcast or a pdf if they buy your book. Keep this special item only for your subscribers.

Use Advertising to Promote Your Book

- ☐ **Use paid sites like BookBub.** Set up an account and list your book under your author profile. Apply to have your book featured in a BookBub Daily Deal. You'll have to discount your book for one day but the site has a large audience.

- ☐ **Get a Kirkus Review.** You can find their submission guidelines [here](.).

- ☐ **Use Amazon Advertising.** You can create a campaign that's budget friendly by using either Sponsored or Lockscreen Ads.

How to Use Live and Online Networking Events to Boost Sales

- ☐ **Host an author Q&A online to promote your book.** Do a blog or social media takeover for someone's site who's in the same niche you're in.

- ☐ **Partner with others.** Find authors releasing a book within the same time period and partner with them for a multi-author event such as a giveaway.

- ☐ **Give a speech.** Offer to host a speech at your Chamber of Commerce, your local library, or a small organization interested in your topic. If your book is about gardening, seek out gardening clubs in your area.

EMAIL MARKETING PLATFORMS

Aweber.com
Anyone that owns their own business needs to be communicating with their subscribers via email. It's used by over 120,000 small businesses and is a proven way to send out newsletters, free products, and products for sell. Aweber has an awesome platform to help you get your merchandise or information out to your subscribers.

GetResponse.com
GetResponse is an autoresponder service that has automation guidelines to let you target your subscribers based on their individual actions, such as them opening an email, clicked a link, made contact changes, or completed transactions.

MailChimp.com
MailChimp utilizes the same service as GetResponse. However, they allow you to send up to 12,000 emails to 2,000 subscribers, for free. Sounds good to me!

Tip: The platforms listed above allow you to send emails out for free (limited amount). My tip to send out more emails is to sign up with all three and take advantage of the free service on them all.

Example: If all three let you send up to 500 emails out for free, if you sign up with all three, you can now send out 1,500 emails!

DICTATE YOUR CONTENT

Transcription is a great way to write an eBook if you have MP3 files or videos that you can turn into content. But what if you don't have anything? What if you know exactly what you want to say, but you don't enjoy typing and find it to be an annoying waste of time?

There's another possibility you could try: dictation. Instead of using content you've already created, you open an app and speak it into it. As you talk, your words are automatically converted into text.

One way to do dictation is by using the recorder on your phone. It will record your vice word for word. Once you're done, you will then need to sit some place quiet and listen to what you've recorded, then manually type everything you hear in your office program.

If you already use office programs regularly, you can open Microsoft Word and look for a microphone button. You have to be signed into the software to see this option. If you're already logged in, simply click on the button. Here's what it looks like:

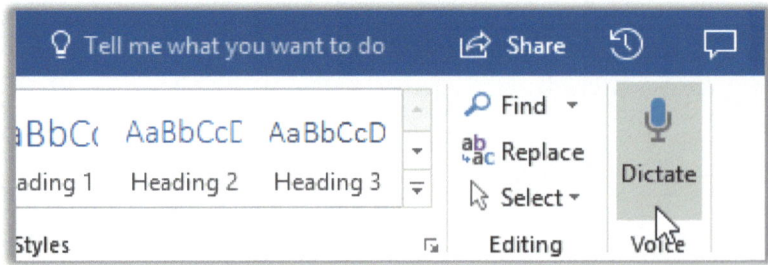

Then you can begin speaking and watching as your text appears. Remember that like many programs, you will need to speak punctuation marks at the end of your sentence.

So when you're done with a thought, you'll say: "How will you know which podcasting microphone you should buy question mark First, you should consider cost period next consider…"

This might seem tedious at first, but after some time passes, you'll get used to it. In fact, you may even find that dictation is easy once you're familiar with how to add punctuation.

If you're not using Microsoft Word, you still have other options for dictation. You can use Google Documents. Simply open a new document and look for "Voice Typing". It's under the tools menu. Here's what the option looks like:

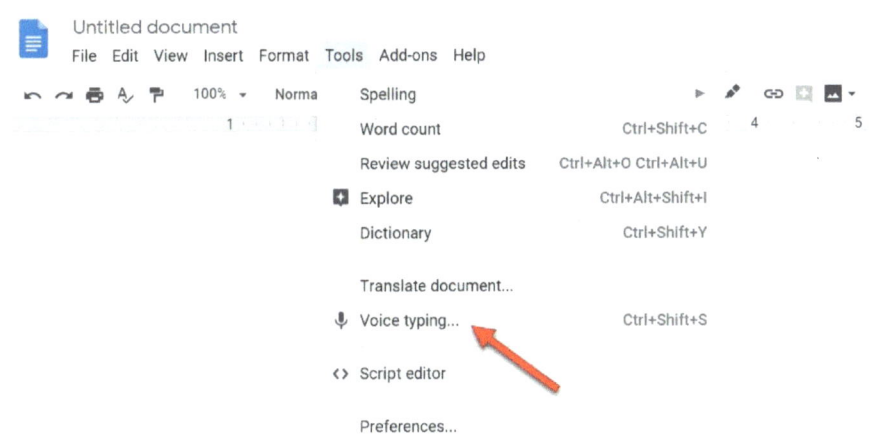

However, Google Documents currently only supports voice typing if you're using the Chrome Browser. Fortunately, **Chrome is free** and easy to install.

If you use Google's voice typing feature, you'll need to speak your punctuation marks just like you do for Microsoft Word and other programs. So don't forget to do that while you're dictating.

You can also use a website like **Dictation.io** or **Speech Notes** to create your book. But keep in mind that you need to be connected to the internet when using either site as they're both online tools.

The cool thing about Dictation.io is that it can translate text from many different spoken languages into your preferred text output. But unfortunately, Dictation is entirely browser based and powered by Google Chrome. That means you'll have to download Chrome if you plan to use the site.

If you need a more robust dictation system and you don't want to pay a small monthly fee, you could purchase **Dragon Naturally Speaking**. Although pricey, this speech recognition software is considered the best on the market and widely trusted around the globe.

For many marketers, dictation is a fun way to write their book. It's often easier to talk about a topic than it is to write down all of your thoughts. If dictation sounds like it might be the answer for you, go ahead and experiment with it!

CHARACTER NAMES

Don't settle when it comes to naming your characters. Names are important because they can portray the strength in your character's role. It can shape their personality, show ethnicity, and even define their future. Okay, maybe not their future, but you get what I mean. All in all, naming your character's can become a huge road block.

Below you will find four ways I come up with my characters' names.

1. **Family & Friends**
   This seems like an easy way to grab up some much needed names for your book. Although some family and friends may find it awesome to have their name in your book, other's may not. The best thing to do is run it by them first just to make sure. It's better to know up front, then find out later. There's nothing worse than going back into a book that's completed to make changes.

2. **Names I Hear**
   I know some people carry a notebook with them everywhere to jot down notes and such, but you can also use an app on your phone to take notes and save them for later. I say this because when I'm outside of the house and I hear a name (or anything of interest), I open my phone and make a note of it. It's quick and easy. The best part about it is that you

can email the list to yourself to have on your computer. How easy is that?

3. Book Of Names

I've gone on Amazon and searched for a book of names and came up with some really great ones. However, I write in many genres, and can't always find a name that I need, especially when I'm writing Urban Fiction. So I sat down and compiled a huge list of names that can be used in many genres, even nick names. You can find this book on Amazon using the link below.

[Writing For Beginners: Names For Your Characters](#)

4. Name Website

[Behind The Name](#) is a website of names and their meaning. It also tells you the gender that the name was used for, where it originated, how it's pronounced, the meaning and its history. The list of names is endless. Basically, it doesn't get any better than this.

In closing, remember to be unique with your names, but not too unique where your reader will have a hard time pronouncing the names you've chosen.

Tip: When you're choosing your character names, don't use names that all start with the same letter. It can confuse the reader and they may mix up who's who. There are plenty of names to choose from, so mix it up in your story.

HOW TO CHOOSE YOUR BOOK'S CATEGORY

The most important thing you can do when uploading your book to a publishing platform is to choose the right categories to place your book in. Here's how to do that the smart way…

List 5 Best-Sellers that Are Like Your Book (Same Genre)

1. _____
2. _____
3. _____
4. _____
5. _____

Check Amazon. In which categories are these best-sellers? *Scroll down to the details on any chosen book and you will see their categories listed.*

1. _____
2. _____
3. _____
4. _____
5. _____

What keywords might describe your eBook? (e.g. thriller, grief, murder, urban, etc.)

Tip: Amazon lets you choose up to 7 keywords so be sure to use them all.

1. _____
2. _____
3. _____
4. _____
5. _____
6. _____
7. _____

Chapter Sections

This sheet is for you to use. It can be edited and saved once you've added your own story.

Chapter 1

Chapterizing is basically breaking down the story into scenes and placing that scene into a chapter. For example, if at the beginning of the story you are talking about waking up, getting dressed, spilling the coffee on your shirt and so forth, all that gets placed under Chapter 1.

Danielle turned over in bed and groaned angrily when she heard her alarm go off. It was Thursday, which usually was her day off, but she had been told to come in to cover for another employee. Kathy, called out at least three times a month and always seemed to dodge pink slips and keep her job. If that was me, I would have gotten the boot with the quickness, Danielle thought, pissed off as she lay there staring at the clock.

Watching the digital numbers click by slowly, she knew she had to get up and start getting ready. With an angry kick, she flung the blanket off her legs and slid to the side of the bed. "This sucks," she mumbled, as she stumbled sleepily towards the bathroom.

Chapter 2

Add text here. Add text here. Add text here. Add text here. Add text here. Add text here. Add text here. Add text here. Add text here. Add text here. Add text here. Add text here.

Chapter 3

And so on…

This is how you should set up your Microsoft Word document to Chapterize your story.

BOOK PUBLISHING LIST

Below is a list of places where you can load/publish your book. Once you have uploaded your book, write in the title, and place a check mark or X in the correct area. There is room for your first 10 books. Good Luck!

NUM	BOOK TITLE	AMAZON	SMASHWORDS	BARNES HIPS	PAYHIP	WEBSITE	INGRAM	COPYRIGHT	GOOGLE PLAY	ACX	DROPBOX		
1.													
2.													
3.													
4.													
5.													
6.													
7.													
8.													
9.													
10.													

CHARACTER/SETTING SHEET

BOOK TITLE _____

SUB TITLE _____

PLACE _____

YEAR _____

SEASON _____

ADD MORE _____

ADD MORE _____

ADD MORE _____

ADD MORE _____

ADD MORE _____

ADD MORE _____

Her Name: **Nick Name:** **Resides:** **Hometown:** **Age:** **Career:** **Kids:** **Single/Married:** **Problem:** **Eye Color:** **Glasses/Contacts:** **Body Shape:** **Height:** **Skin Tone:** **Distinguishing Marks:** **Healthy:** **Hobby:** **Bad Habits:** **Extra Details:**	**His Name:** **Nick Name:** **Resides:** **Hometown:** **Age:** **Career:** **Kids:** **Singled/Married:** **Problem:** **Eye Color:** **Glasses/Contacts:** **Body Shape:** **Height:** **Skin Tone:** **Distinguishing Marks:** **Healthy:** **Hobby:** **Bad Habits:** **Extra Details:**

Her Mother Name:	Her Father Name:
Nick Name:	Nick Name:
Resides:	Resides:
Hometown:	Hometown:
Age:	Age:
Career:	Career:
Kids:	Kids:
Single/Married:	Singled/Married:
Problem:	Problem:
Eye Color:	Eye Color:
Glasses/Contacts:	Glasses/Contacts:
Body Shape:	Body Shape:
Height:	Height:
Skin Tone:	Skin Tone:
Distinguishing Marks:	Distinguishing Marks:
Healthy:	Healthy:
Hobby:	Hobby:
Bad Habits:	Bad Habits:
Extra Details:	Extra Details:

His Mother Name: **Nick Name:** **Resides:** **Hometown:** **Age:** **Career:** **Kids:** **Single/Married:** **Problem:** **Eye Color:** **Glasses/Contacts:** **Body Shape:** **Height:** **Skin Tone:** **Distinguishing Marks:** **Healthy:** **Hobby:** **Bad Habits:** **Extra Details:**	**His Father Name:** **Nick Name:** **Resides:** **Hometown:** **Age:** **Career:** **Kids:** **Singled/Married:** **Problem:** **Eye Color:** **Glasses/Contacts:** **Body Shape:** **Height:** **Skin Tone:** **Distinguishing Marks:** **Healthy:** **Hobby:** **Bad Habits:** **Extra Details:**

Other Characters

Name: **Nick Name:** **Resides:** **Hometown:** **Age:** **Career:** **Kids:** **Single/Married:** **Problem:** **Eye Color:** **Glasses/Contacts:** **Body Shape:** **Height:** **Skin Tone:** **Distinguishing Marks:** **Healthy:** **Hobby:** **Bad Habits:** **Extra Details:**	**Name:** **Nick Name:** **Resides:** **Hometown:** **Age:** **Career:** **Kids:** **Singled/Married:** **Problem:** **Eye Color:** **Glasses/Contacts:** **Body Shape:** **Height:** **Skin Tone:** **Distinguishing Marks:** **Healthy:** **Hobby:** **Bad Habits:** **Extra Details:**

Name: **Nick Name:** **Resides:** **Hometown:** **Age:** **Career:** **Kids:** **Single/Married:** **Problem:** **Eye Color:** **Glasses/Contacts:** **Body Shape:** **Height:** **Skin Tone:** **Distinguishing Marks:** **Healthy:** **Hobby:** **Bad Habits:** **Extra Details:**	**Name:** **Nick Name:** **Resides:** **Hometown:** **Age:** **Career:** **Kids:** **Singled/Married:** **Problem:** **Eye Color:** **Glasses/Contacts:** **Body Shape:** **Height:** **Skin Tone:** **Distinguishing Marks:** **Healthy:** **Hobby:** **Bad Habits:** **Extra Details:**

Name: **Nick Name:** **Resides:** **Hometown:** **Age:** **Career:** **Kids:** **Single/Married:** **Problem:** **Eye Color:** **Glasses/Contacts:** **Body Shape:** **Height:** **Skin Tone:** **Distinguishing Marks:** **Healthy:** **Hobby:** **Bad Habits:** **Extra Details:**	**Name:** **Nick Name:** **Resides:** **Hometown:** **Age:** **Career:** **Kids:** **Singled/Married:** **Problem:** **Eye Color:** **Glasses/Contacts:** **Body Shape:** **Height:** **Skin Tone:** **Distinguishing Marks:** **Healthy:** **Hobby:** **Bad Habits:** **Extra Details:**

Name: Nick Name: Resides: Hometown: Age: Career: Kids: Single/Married: Problem: Eye Color: Glasses/Contacts: Body Shape: Height: Skin Tone: Distinguishing Marks: Healthy: Hobby: Bad Habits: Extra Details:	Name: Nick Name: Resides: Hometown: Age: Career: Kids: Singled/Married: Problem: Eye Color: Glasses/Contacts: Body Shape: Height: Skin Tone: Distinguishing Marks: Healthy: Hobby: Bad Habits: Extra Details:

Name: Nick Name: Resides: Hometown: Age: Career: Kids: Single/Married: Problem: Eye Color: Glasses/Contacts: Body Shape: Height: Skin Tone: Distinguishing Marks: Healthy: Hobby: Bad Habits: **Extra Details:**	Name: Nick Name: Resides: Hometown: Age: Career: Kids: Singled/Married: Problem: Eye Color: Glasses/Contacts: Body Shape: Height: Skin Tone: Distinguishing Marks: Healthy: Hobby: Bad Habits: **Extra Details:**

Congratulations

CONGRATULATIONS ON YOUR PURCHASE!

AS A THANK YOU WE ARE GIFTING YOU WITH THIS ONE TIME COUPON OFFER TO HAVE A EBOOK COVER DESIGNED AT NO COST TO YOU.

TO REDEEM THIS COUPON YOU WILL NEED TO PROVIDE YOUR NAME AND RECEIPT AS PROOF OF PURCHASE BY EMAIL WHEN ASKED.

OR SEND YOUR NAME AND RECEIPT TO THE EMAIL PROVIDED TO RECEIVE YOUR EBOOK COVER!

COVERMESERVICE@YAHOO.COM

OR INBOX THE DESIGNER YOUR PURCHASE INFORMATION ON FACEBOOK!

[Dynasty's Visionary Designs](#)

IF YOU HAVE ANY PURCHASE OR AUTHOR QUESTIONS FEEL FREE TO EMAIL US AT:

COVERMESERVICE@YAHOO.COM

www.ingramcontent.com/pod-product-compliance
Lightning Source LLC
Chambersburg PA
CBHW042003150426
43194CB00002B/107